PICHKA HARAWIKUNA:
Five Quechua Poets

an anthology

Edited and Introduced by
Julio Noriega Bernuy

Translated by
Maureen Ahern

PICHKA HARAWIKUNA:
Five Quechua Poets

an anthology

Edited and Introduced by
Julio Noriega Bernuy

Translated by
Maureen Ahern

Poetry in Indigenous Languages
General Series Editor
Daniel Shapiro

Americas Society
Latin American Literary Review Press
1998

The Latin American Literary Review Press publishes Latin American creative writing under the series title Discoveries, and critical works under the series title Explorations.

Library of Congress Cataloging-in-Publication Data:

Pichka harawikuna : five Quechua poets : an anthology / edited and
    introduced by Julio Noriega Bernuy ; translated by Maureen Ahern.
            p.   cm. -- (Poetry in indigenous languages)
    English, Quechua, and Spanish.
    Includes bibliographical references.
    ISBN 0-935480-98-6
    1. Quechua poetry. I. Noriega Bernuy, Julio. II. Series.
PM6308.6.P53 1998
898'.3231008--dc21   98-37802
                                                      CIP

The Quechua and Spanish versions of these poems were published in *Poesía quechua escrita en el Perú* (Lima: Centro de Estudios y Publicaciones, 1993), edited by Julio Noriega Bernuy.

Cover: *Arbol de la vida* (detail), by Josué Sánchez

The paper used in this publication meets the minimum requirements of the American National Standard for Permanence of Paper for Printed Library Materials Z39.48-1984.◯

Latin American Literary Review Press
121 Edgewood Avenue
Pittsburgh, PA 15218

ACKNOWLEDGMENTS

Grateful acknowledgment is made to the National Endowment for the Arts and the Witter Bynner Foundation for Poetry, Inc., for their generous support of *Pichka Harawikuna: Five Quechua Poets* and *Ül: Four Mapuche Poets* of the Poetry in Indigenous Languages series.

GENERAL EDITOR'S NOTE

Poetry in Indigenous Languages was conceived as a series of chapbooks which would present work by contemporary poets who write in indigenous languages such as Quechua and Mapudungun. These books would be presented in trilingual format—in the indigenous language, in Spanish, and in English—in order to reach general readers, as well as scholars of indigenous and Latin American literatures, throughout the United States.

The project was launched with generous funding from the Witter Bynner Foundation for Poetry, the Consulate General of Chile, and the Ministry of Foreign Affairs of Chile. It was subsequently expanded into a full-fledged book series in order to ensure the highest quality production and the broadest possible distribution for the books. The Latin American Literary Review Press subsequently committed to co-publishing the Quechua and Mapudungun poetry books with funds from the NEA. *Pichka Harawikuna: Five Quechua Poets* is the first title in the series.

Poetry in Indigenous Languages continues the tradition of the Americas Society, formerly the Center for Inter-American Relations, of providing support for the translation of works of Latin American literature. These have included classic texts of the Boom such as Gabriel García Márquez's *One Hundred Years of Solitude*, Julio Cortázar's *Hopscotch*, and José Lezama Lima's *Paradiso*, as well as critical editions of indigenous writing such as *Cantares Mexicanos*, and *Four Masterworks of American Indian Literature*. This series is particularly important in that it will provide significant exposure for the respective writers and for the indigenous cultures they represent.

In addition to the organizations mentioned above, there are many individuals whose dedication and support have been indispensable to this endeavor. I thank Julio Noriega and Maureen Ahern, respectively, the editor and English translator, and the poets represented in this collection: Dida Aguirre, Lily Flores, William Hurtado, Eduardo Ninamango, and Porfirio Meneses. At the Americas Society, I thank Elizabeth A. Beim, Senior Director of Cultural Affairs; Alfred and

Barbara Mac Adam, Editor and Associate Editor of *Review: Latin American Literature and Arts*; and Héctor López, Assistant in the Department of Literature. I also thank Raquel Chang-Rodríguez; Alan Ryan; Sonia Kravajna, at the Witter Bynner Foundation; and Kathleen Ballew. Finally, I express my gratitude to Yvette Miller, Publisher of Latin American Literary Review Press, whose enthusiasm and good will enabled this project to come to fruition.

—Daniel Shapiro
General Series Editor
Director of Literature, Americas Society

CONTENTS

Introduction by Julio Noriega Bernuy   11

Dida Aguirre García   13
Usamanta pikiyaq runa
"Piojito negro" / "Little black louse"   14
"Padre mío" / "My father"   16
"Arbolito flores amarillas" / "Tiny yellow flowers"   18
Apu Wamani
"Relampagueamos" / "Let's strike like lightning"   20
Quechua
Usamanta pikiyaq runa
"Yana usacha"   22
"Taytallay"   23
"Sapan waranwaychallay"   24
Apu Wamani
"Wakrillanchikmi"   25

Lily Flores Palomino   27
Pollerita roja / Red Skirt   28
de Proyectil / *from* Projectile   30
Todo se va consumando / Everything's Ending   32
Incineración / Conflagration   36
Quechua
Puka pulleracha   38
Phawaq titi   39
Tukuy imapas tukukushanñan   40
K'añay   42

William Hurtado de Mendoza   43
Canción para que aprendas / A Learning Song   44
Carta / A Letter   48
Quechua
Yachanaykipaq taki   58
Qelqa   60

Eduardo Ninamango Mallqui   65
de Tormenta (1, 2, 3, 5) / *from* Storm (1, 2, 3, 5)   66
Quechua
Pukutay (1, 2, 3, 5)   74

Porfirio Meneses Lazón   79
¿Quién? / Who?   80
Vete ya, señor / Get Out, Señor   82
Pregonero agreste / Rustic Crier   84
Sandalia de indias / Indian Woman's Sandal   86
Quechua
¿Pim chay?   88
Ripuyña, tayta   89
Qapariku   90
Paqu kitikunapa usutan   91

Bibliography   93

Biographical information   95

INTRODUCTION*

The five contemporary Quechua poets represented in this collection share similar life experiences. They are all natives of either the southern or central regions of Andean Peru. After learning strategies for surviving the conflict between their traditional Quechua world and the modern Western one, in their native towns as well as in Lima, where they migrated, they are now dedicated to university teaching. As a result of their dual cultural ties, these writers not only identify themselves as Andean migrants, writers in exile, and natives bilingual in Quechua and Spanish, but also as poets who began to write first in Spanish but later, more naturally, in Quechua.

Although their poetry still resounds with the dissonant echoes of distinct literary traditions in conflict with the modes and aims of cultural modernization, the Quechua poetics they have introduced is neither Indian nor Indigenist but one informed by the poets' migrant identity. In this poetics, the subject is not an isolated or idealized Indian, but a mythic hero, a kind of Quechua Odysseus who, as an orphan and a wanderer, takes up the quest to reconquer the city from the country and the written tradition from the oral one. The poetic text becomes a type of experimental writing about Andean myths and rituals. When the texts do not transcribe modern versions of millennial oral tales, usually their language and discourse succeed in transmitting the voices of Indian ancestors and gods. Furthermore, the very act of poetic creation is performed as a ritual of re-encounter between the author and her or his original world—a cultural practice which, by adapting itself to the precepts of a traditional Quechua cosmovision, transforms literature into a myth or utopia that makes the impossible possible: the reconstruction of the Andean world in a universal dimension through the re-establishment of the interrupted dialogue between Andean migrants and their ancestral gods.

Within these heterogeneous currents, each migrant poet is distinguished by her or his own style and ideology. If Dida Aguirre and Eduardo Ninamango appear to share similar concerns, it is because both poets practice a kind of poetic anthropology. Aguirre is attracted to testimony

*Translated by Maureen Ahern

as a means to denounce the many forms of violence against the Quechua people over the centuries, including the destruction or forced removal of entire villages. Ninamango consolidates the dual and rootless vision of the Andean migrant who tragically struggles between apocalyptic destruction and utopian revolution. The colloquial tone, nostalgic and intimate, that both Lily Flores and Porfirio Meneses evoke in their poetry best finds its pitch and marks its own melody when their poems are read within the context of Quechua songs. Meneses's poems can be understood in terms of the *harawi*, the indigenous farewell lament of human beings who have been ripped from their cosmos. Flores's poems can be understood in terms of the traditional *wayno*, whose performance requires not only particular dialogue, metaphors, and similes in all their polyphonic dimensions, but also a feminine tone of voice to guarantee its authenticity. Finally, William Hurtado has created, from the many images originating in the Andean migrant experience, the poetic image of a leader and messianic prophet to indigenous people in their struggle for definitive liberation.

Julio Noriega Bernuy
University of Notre Dame

DIDA AGUIRRE GARCIA
(Pampas, Huancavelica, 1953)

Dida Aguirre García studied Social Work at the Universidad Nacional Mayor de San Marcos in Lima and at the Universidad Inca Garcilaso de la Vega, also in Lima. She is now a professor at the Universidad Daniel Alcides Carrión in Cerro de Pasco. She has published poems in Quechua and Spanish in journals in Peru (*Kilka* and *Carrión*), Mexico (*Cantos de los Colores*) and Colombia (*Zumo Sumo*). She has published a collection of bilingual poetry, *Arcilla* (Lima: Lluvia Editores, 1989), which consists of Quechua poems with accompanying Spanish versions, and poems written in Quechua-influenced Spanish. Aguirre García is also the author of an unpublished book of poems, and is presently compiling a collection of stories and Quechua riddles.

USAMANTA PIKIYAQ RUNA

Piojito negro
piojito blanco

qué estás haciendo
    escondido

    ¡vivamente
transfórmate en pulga!

cuando hay maqta
¡existe pueblo!
cuando hay pasña
¡basural! dice el dicho

    Pero
con sus pies de pulga
    todos
los maqtas con sus pasñas
    son capaces
de conducir el pueblo
    por eso
¡hombre piojo
    de prisa
conviértete en pulga!

USAMANTA PIKIYAQ RUNA*

Little black louse
Little white louse

what are you doing
        hiding there?

        Quickly
turn into a flea!

When they're guys
they're a people,
when they're gals,
rubbish, or so goes the saying.

        But
with their flea feet
        all
the guys with their gals
        can lead
their people.
        So
louse-man,
        hurry up!
Turn into a flea!

Usamanta pikiyaq runa: Awakened man

PADRE MIO

Padre mío
padre viejecito
tú
sí estás sabiendo
en tu cabecita blanca
de esta vida
la convivencia.

Hermanado con la tierra
como
una roca robusta
de raíces poderosas
te
asomas.

Tú
sí estás sabiendo
de hombres que existen
como
piojos y carroñas
que
no tienen donde fijarse
como
piedras redondas
que no echan raíces.

Padre mío
padre viejecito
tú
sí estás sabiendo.

MY FATHER

My Father,
dear ancient Father,
You
do know
in that white head of yours
about
living together.

Living like a brother
to the earth
like
a strong rock
with powerful roots
You gaze out.

You
do know about
men who exist
like
lice and rotting flesh,
loose
like
round stones
that grow no roots.

My Father,
dear ancient Father,
Yes,
you do know.

ARBOLITO FLORES AMARILLAS

Arbolito flores amarillas
dice lloras solito
entre las chamanas y las tayas
de loma
en loma
así no lloraremos

no
a nuestros
trapos hilachándose
¡como ríos temibles
nuestras lágrimas hervirán!

¡gritando!
¡llamando!

iremos ya,
viajaremos ya
llevando tristeza
llevando pobreza hermana
de la mano
iremos
en turba
en masa

nos iremos ya,
viajaremos ya

para que esta tierra madrecita
vuelva a vivir
con nosotros
¡vámonos ya
como águilas y galgas
hirviendo!

TINY YELLOW FLOWERS

Tiny yellow flowers,
Everyone knows that you're crying alone
among *chamanas* and *tayas**
from knoll
to knoll.
Let's not cry.

No, let's not cry
for
our unravelling rags.
Our tears will boil
like fearful rivers!

Shouting
calling

Let's get going!
Let's travel on.
Carrying sorrow
taking sister poverty
by the hand,
we'll go
as a mob
a crowd.

Let's get going!
Let's travel on.

So our dear Mother Earth
may return to live
with us.
Let's go!
Like eagles and boulders
thundering.

* *Chamana* is a shrub, and *taya* is a tree, both indigenous to the high Andean regions.

APU WAMANI

Relampagueamos
desde el oscuro hoyo
de la madre tierra
por ser pueblos
raigambre de
rocas,
y de aquellos
agusanados nubosos
(locos)
cabezas de hueso
hasta sus sesos hirviendo
lo lavaremos
si
como la piedra redonda
no echan raíces
hombres diablos
botas rojas
¡ay!
padrecito padre wamani
tú sí estás sabiendo
cual es el destino final de
nuestro camino
en esta tierra.

APU WAMANI*

Let's strike like lightning!
from the dark cavity
of Mother Earth,
because we're people
rooted in rocks,
and we'll wash
those
wormridden cloudy
insane
boney heads
right up to
their boiling brains.
As if a round stone
rootless
devil men
red boots
Oh yeah!
Dear Father Wamani,
yes, you know
the final destiny
of our road
upon this earth.

* *Apu Wamani*: Father Mountain God

USAMANTA PIKIYAQ RUNA*

Yana usacha
yuraq usacha

imatataq ruwanki
    pakarayaspa

¡vivuta pikiyay!

maqta kaptin
    llaqta

pasña kaptin
    qopa pata
    ninkum

piki chakichallan
llapa maqta pasñanwan
    llaqtata
puririchinku

    chaymi
usamanta runa

¡vivuta pikiyay!

*"Piojito negro"

TAYTALLAY*

Taytallay
tayta aukis
qamqa yachallachkankim
yuraq soqo
umachaykipi

kay vida kausaqta.

Allpawan
waqechakuykuspam
raku sapisapa
qaqa rumillaña wateqamunki

qamqa yachallachkankim
usa jina, aqchi jina
runakuna
kausasqanta

mana maypi tiyariq
muyru rumi jina
mana sapiyuq kaq

taytallay
tayta aukis
qamqa
yachallachkankim.

*"Padre mío"

SAPAN WARANWAYCHALLAY*

Sapan waranwaychallay
sapachallaykis
waqakullanki˙
chamana taya waqtakunapi

amaya
ama chaynaqa waqakusunchu
wakcha lliki llikanchikta
¡manchapa mayu jinam
weqenchik timpuy
timpukunqa!
¡qaparikuspa!
¡qayarikuspa!

ripukullasunña
pasakullasunña

lliu llaqui
wakchakunata
aysarikuykuspa
chipay
chipaymi
ripukullasun
pasakullasun
kay mamapacha allpachallanchik
ñoqallanchikwan
kausarinampaq

¡pasasunña ripucusunña
kuchpallaña ankallaña

timpukullaspa!

*"Arbolito flores amarillas"

APU WAMANI*

Wakrillanchikmi
kay tuta uku pachamanta
qaqa sapiyuq llaqtakuna
kaspa
kuruyasqa
puyuyasqa
tullu umankumantam
ñotqontapas
timpuruspa mayllarusun
chay
muyru rumi jina mana sapiyuq
supay puka
butas runakunapata
¡ay! taytachallay tayta
wamani
qamqa
yachallachkankim
may
ñanchallanchik
kay
pachapi kananta.

*"Relampagueamos"

LILY FLORES PALOMINO
(Abancay, Apurimac, 1937)

Lily Flores Palomino completed her primary education in Arequipa and her secondary and universitary studies in Lima. In 1987 she received the Cantuta de Oro Prize and the National Urpicha de Plata Prize of the First Festival of Andean Authors and Composers. She is author of three Quechua poetry collections: *Troj de poema queshua castellano* (Lima: César Lanegra, 1971), *Phawaq titi* (Lima: Editorial Perú, 1985), and *Waqalliq-takin/ Tañido de campanas* (Lima: CONCYTEC, 1989).

POLLERITA ROJA

¿Eres flor o mujer,
con esa hermosa pollerita?
¿Amapola o clavelina,
con esa tu cara roja?

Soy mujer, señor,
soy joven, señora.

Pollerita roja.
¿Perdiz o vicuña eres,
por qué apareces y desapareces?
¿eres venado o vizcacha
que tan esquiva eres?

Imposible señor,
imposible señora.

Pollerita roja.
Si mujer eres, acércate a mí,
si flor eres yo te arrancaré,
y si eres venado o perdiz
con mi querer te enlazaré
y tus alitas cortaré.

Si tú quieres, mujer
si tú quieres, flor
flor o mujer,
venado o perdiz
lo que tú quieras soy
pollerita roja soy.

RED SKIRT

You there
with that handsome skirt,
Are you a flower or a woman?
With that red face there,
are you a poppy or a carnation?

I'm a woman, Señor.
I'm a young man, Señora.

Hey there, red skirt.
Are you a partridge or a vicuña?
Appearing and disappearing.
Are you a deer or a *vizcacha*?
You're so shy.

Impossible, Señor.
Impossible, Señora.

Hey there, red skirt.
If you're a woman, come close to me.
If you're a flower, I'll pluck you.
Or if you're a deer or a partridge
I'll tie you up with my love
and trim your little wings.

I'm a woman, if you like,
I'm a flower, if you like.
Flower or woman
deer or partridge
I'm whatever you like,
I'm a red skirt.

* *Vizcacha*: Rodent indigenous to the Andes

PROYECTIL

Si pudiera ser la bala
que escapa del fusil
que dispara el soldado:

Iría en busca
de los amantes de la guerra
y traspasaría sin piedad
su rocoso corazón.

Después al río me lanzaría
para que nunca más
me vuelvan a disparar.
¡Pero sólo soy mujer!

Si fuera la espada
con que se reta al enemigo

Cortaría sin temor,
con mi filo reluciente,
la cabeza de los masacristas
que degüellan con sadismo
a las madres y a los niños.

Después penetraría en la tierra
reflejando, ondulante,
de donde nunca más
nadie me levante.
¡Pero sólo soy bandera!

Si fuera el proyectil
que sale del cañón
para dar fin al combatiente

Iría en busca
de los que mandan la encarnizada
y les cortaría el aire que respiran . . .

PROJECTILE

If I were the bullet
shot from the gun
the soldier fires,

I'd go in search
of the lovers of war
and pierce their rough hearts
without mercy.

Then I'd fling myself into the river
so they could never
fire me again.
But I'm only a woman!

If I were the sword
that challenges the enemy

With my shining blade
I'd fearlessly slash off
the heads of the assassins
that sadistically
behead mothers and children.

Then, reflecting and waving,
I'd pierce the earth
where no one
would ever raise me.
But I'm only a flag!

If I were the projectile
flung from a cannon
to annihilate the enemy

I'd search out
those who order slaughter
and cut off the very air they breathe . . .

TODO SE VA CONSUMANDO

Todo, todo se va consumando
ya nada es bueno:

Las Madres no quieren parir, lo evitan
los niños no ríen, lloran
los pajarillos no trinan, gimen
los ríos no suenan, se lamentan
y los árboles, ya no dan frutos.

Ya todo se va consumando
porque los hombres ya no tienen:
Sincero amor y ternura,
con las madres y los niños.

Porque los hombres ya no escuchan:
el trinar de los pajarillos.
Porque los árboles ya no beben
la dulce agua de los ríos.

Ya todo se va consumando
porque los hombres ya no son hermanos,
son tribus salvajes de pirañas
que se odian y se matan.

Y todo se va consumando
porque hay desigualdad humana:
hay hambre hay guerra
hay paganismo y crueldad,
hay orfandad interior
hay llanto y dolor . . .

¡Pero no están consumados:
el tronar de los cañones
el reventar de las balas
y el sonar de las espadas!

EVERYTHING'S ENDING

Everything's ending.
Nothing's good anymore.

Mothers don't give birth, they abort.
Children don't laugh, they cry.
Birds don't trill, they whimper.
Rivers don't roar, they wail.
Trees no longer bear.

Everything's ending
because men no longer bear
genuine love or tenderness
for mothers or children.

Because men no longer listen
to the trill of birds.
Because trees no longer drink
fresh water from rivers.

Everything's ending.
Men are no longer brothers
but savage tribes of piranha
who hate and murder each other.

Everything's ending
because there's inequality,
famine and war,
paganism and cruelty,
inner orphanhood,
sobbing and sorrow . . .

But the roar of cannons
exploding shells
and clashing swords
are not extinguished!

Y no serán aplacados
porque nadie lo sofoca
todos están armados . . .
Para luchar por sus fronteras . . .

Así, así de pie como reluciente acero
están las balas del alma
de mis hermanos de batalla,
los poetas . . . que disparan al universo,
en esta guerra, del mundo terrenal.

They'll not be placated
because no one puts them out.
They're all armed
and fighting for their borders.

So here, shining like steel,
are the bullets of the souls
of my brothers in the struggle,
the poets . . . who take aim at the universe
in this war on earth.

INCINERACION

Cuando yo muera
otra vez polvo seré,
sepulcro sin cadáver
cadáver sin cuerpo
tumba sin cruz
sin visitas ni flores
ceniza esparcida
sobre el mar
y las rosas
perenne estaré.

CONFLAGRATION

When I die
I'll turn to dust again;
tomb without a corpse,
corpse without a body,
grave without a cross,
no visitors no flowers.
I'll be
ashes scattered
on the sea
and everblooming roses.

PUKA PULLERACHA*

¿T'ikachu warmichu kanki
chay, sumaj pullerachaykiwan?
¿Amapolachu, clavelinachu
chay puka uyaykiwan?

Warmin kakuni, taytay,
sipasmi kakuni, mamay.

Puka pulleracha.
¿Yutuchu, vicuñachu kanki,
chaytaj, rijurinkitaj chinkakunkitaj?
¿luychuchu, viscachachu kanki
chaytaj, qayrallana kanki?

Manapuni hinachu, taytay,
manapuni hinachu, mamay.

Puka pulleracha.
Warmi kaspaqa, ñoqaman asuyamuy,
t'ika kajtikiqa, ñoqa t'ipisayki,
luychupas, yutupis kajtikiqa
munakuyniywan lasusayki
raphrachaykitataj kuchusayki.

Munajtikiqa warmi
munajtikiqa t'ika
t'ikapas, warmipas
luychupas, yutupas
ima munasqaykin kani
puka pullerachan kani.

*Pollerita roja

PHAWAQ TITI*

Waya wisaq ñitisqan
runa wañuchinaq toqasqan
phawaq titi kayman chayqa.

Khuyaylla auqanakuy munaqtacha
mashkaq riyman
mana llakirikuspataq, haykuruyman
qaqa sonqonman.

Chaymantataq mayuman
chanqayakamuyman, manaña kayk'aq,
t'oqyachiwanankupaj.
¡Hinanaypaqtaq warmilla kani!

Cheqninakuqkunaq auqanan,
k'illkamanta kuchuna kayman chayqa.

Mana mancharikuspacha willuyman
k'ancharishaq kauchiywan
nak'achukunaq umanta
asispa mamakunata, wawakunata
nak'asqankumanta.

Chaymantataq, k'ancharispa, q'ewirikuspa
allpawan millp'uchikuyman,
mañana pipas
uqariwananpaq.
¡Hinanaypaqtaq unanchaylla kani!

Nina toqaq kañonmanta
phawaq titi, auqaqkuna tukuq hina
kayman chayqa.

Mashkamuymanchá
aycha kuchu kamachiqkunata,
samayninta mukichinaypaq . . .

*Proyectil

TUKUY IMAPAS TUKUKUSHANÑAN*

Tukuypas tukuy imapas tukukushanñan
manañan imapas allinchu.

Mamakunapas manañan, wachayta
munankuchu, amachakuspa
warmakunapas, manañan asinkuchu,
waqallankuñan
tiutichakunapas, manañan takinkuchu,
iqepallankuñan
mayukunapas manañan qaparinchu,
llakillankuñan
sach'akunapas manañan rurunchu.

Ñan tukuy imapas tukukushanñan
manañan runakunapa kanchu
cheqaq munakuynin, wayllukuynimpas
wawakunayoq, mamakunapas.

Manañan runakunaqa uyarinkuchu
tiutikunaq takinta,
manañan sach'akuna uphyanchu
mayukunaq miski yakunta.

Ñan tukuy imapas tukukushanña
runakunapas manañan turantinchu kanku
kankuqa: salqa llaqta phiña challwakunan
cheqninakuspa, wañuchinakuqkuna.

Tukuy imapas tukukushanñataqmi
rakinasqa runakunapas kaqtin
yarqaywan, auqanakuyllawanña kaqtin
nanakuq, sasa ñakariyllaña kaqtin
waqaytaq llakitaq, kaqtin
ch'usaq sonqo kay piwan.

*Todo se va consumando

Ichaqa manan tukukunchu
toqyaq, atun killkaq kununuyninqa
wanku titi phawachip, killkupapas
k'uchuq killku, ch'eq ch'eqyaynimpas.

Manataqmi thaninqakuchu
mana pipa amachakuqtin
lliupas auqana haphtayurqakaman
llaqtanku chimpa amachakunankupaq.

Shayna shayna, llipipiq killka hina sayasqan
kashan, auqanakuq turaykunapa
nunankuq toqyachisqankuqa
harawikunaq, pachantimpaq, toqyachiyninqa
kay teqsi muyu allpaq, auqanakuynimpi.

K'AÑAY*

Ñoqa wañuqtiyqa
yapamantan allpa kasaq,
mana wañusqayoq t'oqo
ch'usaq wañusqa
mana cruzniyoq p'ampana
mana watukayniyoq, mana t'ikayoq
Mama qochapi
wisñisqa uspa
t'ikakunapiwan
wiñaypaq kasaq.

*Incineración

WILLIAM HURTADO DE MENDOZA
(Cuzco, 1946)

William Hurtado de Mendoza is a bilingual poet and professor at the Universidad Agraria de La Molina in Lima. During the military regime of Juan Velazco, he was an editor of *Cronicawan*, a Quechua-language newspaper. He began writing poetry in Spanish in 1967, and in Quechua, four years later. Since then, he has published *Yanapaq jailli* (Lima: Ediciones Martínez, 1971), *Yachaynakipaq taki/Canción para que aprendas* (Lima: Perugraph Editores, 1977), *Mateo Llaqta* (Lima: Lluvia Editores, 1987), and *Poesía quechua: selección para niños* (Lima: Lluvia Editores, 1990).

CANCION PARA QUE APRENDAS

I

Antes que tus ojos
conocieran que hay una noche
tras cada día.

Antes que tus labios
nombraran
lo que tus manos alcanzaban.

Antes que tus pasos
desataran dolorosos
caminos sin fin y sin estada.

Antes que tu razón
encontrara
la columna de esta tierra.

Y mucho antes aún
que pudieras conocer
el hinchado esfuerzo de los hombres.

Ya tú aprendiste
ese sí
de la obediencia.

A LEARNING SONG

I

Before your eyes
knew there was night
behind day.

Before your lips
named what your hands
touched.

Before your steps
set out upon
painful
endless roads without a stay.

Before your reason
found
the backbone of this earth.

And long before
you could understand
the highblown efforts of men,

You had already learned
that obedient Yes.

II

De hoy y hasta mañana
te enseño en este canto
a gritar NO, para negarte.

De hoy y hasta mañana
te enseño en este canto
a rebelarte.

De hoy y hasta mañana
te enseño en este canto
a agigantarte.

De hoy y hasta mañana
te enseño en este canto
a ensangrentar el firmamento.

De hoy y hasta mañana
a volver a ti
te enseño en este canto.

II

As of today and tomorrow
through this song I'll teach you
to shout NO, to refuse.

As of today and tomorrow
through this song I'll teach you
to rebel.

As of today and tomorrow
Through this song I'll teach you
to become a giant.

As of today and tomorrow
through this song I'll teach you
to bloody the sky.

As of today and tomorrow
through this song I'll teach you
to turn to yourself.

CARTA

I

Te escribo
antes que el sol
se adormezca en sus cenizas.

Antes que el fuego
sea carbón oscuro y negro.

Antes que el día
pierda su rastro tras la noche.

Antes que el arco iris
forje frío en la llovizna.

Antes que los relámpagos
estén nevando entre las nubes.

Antes que el granizo
llore entre los vientos.

Y mucho antes aún
que el frío duela en el corazón.

Te escribo urgente
sin que sepa el viento
para que nadie se humille.

A LETTER

I

I'm writing to you
before the sun
dozes in its ashes.

Before fire
becomes blackest charcoal.

Before day
loses its way behind the night.

Before the rainbow
casts cold into drizzle.

Before lightning
starts snowing among the clouds.

Before hail
wails through the winds.

And long before
cold aches in your heart.

I'm writing to you urgently
without the wind's knowing,
so no one will be humbled.

II

Te escribo
antes que mi quena
cante su cuajarón de sangre.

Antes que este canto
ponga penumbra a la congoja.

Antes que este himno
sea un espectro moribundo.

Antes que mis nervios
se vuelquen desasidos,

Antes que mis huesos
se entumezcan en la muerte.

Antes que mis ojos
se calcinen en su llanto.

Y antes aún que mi altura
busque un cayado,

Te escribo urgente
sin que sepa el viento
para que nadie se humille.

II

I'm writing to you
Before my *quena*
sings clotted blood.

Before this song
casts a shadow upon anguish.

Before this hymn
becomes a dying ghost.

Before my tendons
lose their tension.

Before my bones
are numbed by death.

Before my eyes
turn to stone from sobbing.

Even before my height
seeks a staff.

I'm writing to you urgently
without the wind's knowing
so no one will be humbled.

III

Te escribo
para que la muerte
no nazca de la esperanza.

Para que no se aquieten
las llagas sobre las piedras.

Para que la sangre
no se enferme en la tristeza.

Y para que el dolor
no se postre en su dolencia.

Te escribo urgente
sin que sepa el viento
para que nadie se humille.

III

I'm writing you
so death will
not be born of hope.

So the scars
on stones won't fade.

So blood
is not tainted by sorrow.

So pain
is not overcome in its ache.

I'm writing to you urgently
so the wind doesn't know
so no one will be humbled.

IV

Te escribo urgente
en el camino de todas las estrellas.

Para que mañana llegue a tu corazón
con su ropaje de nubes.

Para que tus manos desaten
la trama que le puso el viento.

Para que tus brasas abriguen
lo que cubren las heladas.

Para que tu fuego acaricie
lo que tejieron las nevadas.

Para que tus manos zurzan
lo que han roto los inviernos.

Para que tus cantos unan
la congoja de los pobres.

IV

I'm writing to you urgently
along the starry roadway.

So tomorrow reaches your heart
in its garment of clouds.

So your hands loosen
the knot the wind tied.

So your embers warm
whatever frost covers.

So your flames caress
the fabric of snowy peaks.

So your hands darn
what winters have torn.

So your songs gather
the grief of the poor.

V

Si cualquier día
alguien por mí te pregunta,

sólo esta parte
en nuestro nombre responde:

Diles que soy yo,
diles que te he escrito en el viento
para que nadie se humille.

V

And if someday someone asks you
about me,

only this
responds for us:

Tell them that I'm the one
who wrote to you on the wind
so no one will be humbled.

YACHANAYKIPAQ TAKI*

I

Manaraq ñawiyki
p'unchaymanta
sapa tutanta riqsishaqtin.

Manaraq simiyki
makiykiq tarpasqanta
sutinta churashaqtin.

Manaraq thaskiyniyki
mana tukukuq ñanta
sasawan paskashaqtin.

Manaraq yuyayniyki
kay pachaq saywanta
tarishaqtin.

Manaraq qanpaq
runaq punkillikusqan
riqsisqa kashaqtinraq.

Ñan qanqa
yacharankiña
chay ari nispa kasukuyta

*Canción para que aprendas

II

Kunanmanta paqarinmanmi
manan niyta
kay takiypi yachachiyki.

Kunanmanta paqarinmanmi
sayariyta
kay takiypi yachachiyki.

Kunanmanta paqarinmanmi
hatunyayta
kay takiypi yachachiyki.

Kunanmanta paqarinmanmi
hanaq pacha yawarchayta
kay takiypi yachachiyki.

Kunanmanta paqarinmanmi
qanman kutiriyta
kay takiypi yachachiyki.

QELQA*

I

Qelqamuykin
manaraq inti
usphanpi puñushaqtin.

Manaraq nina yana
k'illinsapi wañushaqtin.

Manaraq p'unchay
tutanpi chinkashaqtin.

Manaraq k'uychi
parapi chirishaqtin.

Manaraq illapa
phuyupi ritishaqtin.

Manaraq chikchi
wayrapi waqashaqtin.

Manaraq chiripas
sunqoypi nanashaqtin.

Usqhaylla qelqamuyki
mana wayraq yachasqallan
ama pipas k'umunanpaq.

*Carta

II

Qelqamuykin
manaraq qenay
t'aka yawarta takishaqtin.

Manaraq harawiyniy
llakita llanthushaqtin.

Manaraq hayllisqay
wañuypi ayayashaqtin.

Manaraq hank'uy
kacharikuq usushaqtin.

manaraq tulluy
tulluyaspa wañushaqtin.

Manaraq ñawiy
waqasqanpi ninayashaqtin.

Manaraq sayayniypas
tawnanta mashkhashaqtin

Usqhaylla qelqamuyki
mana wayraq yachasqallan
ama pipas k'umunanpaq.

III

Qelqamuykin
Amaña wañuy
suyaymanta phutunanpaq.

Amaña k'iri
rumipi takyananpaq.

Amaña yawar
llakipi unqonanpaq.

Amaña nanaypas
nanayninpi unphunanpaq.

Usqhayllan qelqamuyki
mana wayraq yachasqallan
ama pipas k'umunanpaq.

IV

Ch'askaq purisqanpin
usqhaylla qelqamuyki.

Paqarin phuyupi p'achallisqa
sunqoykiman chayananpaq.

Wayraq allwisqanta
makiyki pashkananpaq.

qasaq qollmusqanta
sansayki p'istunanpaq.

Rit'iq awasqanta
ninayki lulunanpaq.

Chiri mit'aq llik'isqanta
sirk'ayki sirananpaq.

Runaq llakisqanta
takiyki huñunanpaq.

V

Paqta pipas
tapurikunman.

Kayllata sutinchispi
willarqokuy.

Nuqa kasqayta niykuy,
willariy,wayrapi ushqhaylla qelqasqayta
ama pipas k'umunanpaq.

EDUARDO NINAMANGO MALLQUI
(Huancayo, 1947)

Eduardo Ninamango Mallqui obtained a bachelor's degree in Hispanic literatures from the Universidad Nacional Mayor de San Marcos de Lima, and a master's degree from the Pontificia Universidad Católica del Perú. For the past few years he has been a professor at the Universidad Nacional del Centro del Perú, in Huancayo. He is the author of *Pukutay/ Tormenta* (Lima: Tarea, 1982), a three-part poetry collection. His poems have also appeared in journals including *Haraui* (no. 33-34, Lima, Sept.-Dec. 1972; no. 40, July 1974) and *Wanka* (Bilingual Journal of Linguistics and Literature, no. 1, Huancayo, UNCP, 1983).

TORMENTA

1

El dolor está llegando a los pueblos
como tormenta de sangre. Estoy
gritando a los abuelos
para que abandonen su morada
y traigan
la sangre de los antiguos dioses.
Tiembla el corazón de la tierra
tiembla el hambre que no tiene barriga
porque la vida es dura,
dura como la sequía que azota a los pueblos
y deja sin una gota de lluvia
a los animales que mueren en el campo
a los árboles que agitan sus ramas
y caen al suelo
como ave herida,
a las gramíneas
que ya no florecerán,
sin que el hombre,
viejo diseñador de historias,
de arcillas,
pueda detener el fuego de la lluvia.

STORM

1

Pain is reaching the people
like a bloodstorm. I'm
shouting to the wise ancestors
to leave their dwelling places
and bring
the blood of the ancient gods.
Heart of earth trembles.
Hunger without a belly trembles
because life is rough,
as rough as the drought that whips the towns,
leaving no rain,
so animals die in the field,
trees shake their branches
and fall to the ground
like wounded birds,
and plants
stop blooming,
while man,
that old designer of stories
and clay,
cannot stop the fire of rain.

2

Los hombres de la tierra sufren
y en sus manos ensangrentadas
nace un dios desconocido,
mientras su infancia camina por las calles
buscando un pedazo de pan;
    los wamanis
viejos cóndores de las montañas
están haciendo bailar a la tierra,
también a los árboles, a las piedras
con grito de voces que nace del río.
Los humanos,
    los pájaros
y todos los seres del universo
    detienen su pena
porque el cielo se agita
    y tiñe su cara
como tormenta de lluvia
como árbol de vida
    dejando caer
flechas de fuego
a los ojos del águila
que huye convertido en ceniza ardiente.

2

Men suffer here on earth
and in their bloody hands
an unknown god is born,
while their abandoned children walk the streets
looking for a crust of bread.
    The *wamanis*,
those old mountain condors,
are making earth dance,
and trees and stones too,
with shouts that rise from the river.
Human beings,
    the birds
and all beings in the universe
    halt hurting,
because the sky shakes
    and darkens its face
like a rainstorm
or a tree of life
    dropping
arrows of fire
into the eyes of the eagle
that flees transformed to burning ash.

3

Porque la tierra ya no es virgen,
tampoco nuestra,
las palomas están dejando su lamento
en el manantial donde las mariposas lloran.
Escucha hermano,
        no es tiempo de llorar,
escucha la voz de los abuelos
que gritan desde el corazón de los cerros
porque ya llega nuestra tormenta de lluvia,
no llores tanto porque mi corazón duele,
como el cóndor que grita en las nieves,
como el toro que defiende su pampa
como tú,
dios de la tierra
que ya no quieres beber la sangre
de las vicuñas que mueren de sed y hambre.
Escucha hermano
        no es tiempo de llorar
la tierra volverá a ser nuestra
porque la tormenta de lluvia ya viene,
viene la tormenta de lluvia
a nuestro pueblo
trayendo peces dorados, celestes
como el cielo donde bailan nuestros abuelos.

3

Because the land is no longer virgin
nor is it ours,
doves drop their lament
into the spring where butterflies weep.
Listen, brother,
　　　it's no time for weeping,
listen to the voices of the wise ancestors
that scream from the heart of the peaks
because now our rainstorm is arriving.
Don't cry so much because my heart aches,
like the condor screaming across the snow,
like the bull defending his pampa,
like you,
earth god,
who no longer wants to drink the blood
of vicuñas dying of hunger and thirst.
Listen, brother,
　　　it's no time for weeping.
The land will be ours once again
because now the rainstorm is reaching
our town,
bringing golden fish, as blue
as the sky where our ancestors danced.

5

Ya no es posible vieja mazorca
volver a tus tierras vírgenes y milagrosas
jugar en la lluvia,
        reír en las tardes frías;
contemplar el vuelo de los cóndores
porque eres un dios en pena
que ahoga su lamento en la coca
y pinta pájaros en la cara del cielo.
        Ya no es posible
buscar lo que era mío
tampoco sentarse en el regazo de mi madre
y ver que la noche llegaba lentamente
a los corazones,
        porque eres un dios en pena
que grita sus alas en el río
y expresa tristeza en las nubes,
mientras busco mi infancia
        eterno
más eterno que tus aguas,
        dulce
como cuando nací entre alisos y retamas.

5

Venerable corn,
I can no longer
return to your wondrous virgin fields,
play in the rain,
        laugh in the cold afternoons
or watch the condors fly,
because you are a grieving god,
drowning his sorrow in coca
and painting doves across the face of the sky.
        I can no longer
search for what was mine
because I can no longer sit
on my mother's lap,
watching how night creeps slowly
from the heart,
        because you are a grieving god,
beating his wings across the river,
expressing his sadness in clouds
while I search for my eternal
        childhood,
more eternal than your
        fresh waters
when I was born among trees
where doves scatter from their nests.

PUKUTAY*

1

Llaqtakunamansi yawar pukutay qina
nanay chayachkan.
Machu taitanchikunatas
qaparispa qayani
wasinchikta saqeychik
ñawpa apuchikunapa yawarninta
aparimuychik nispa.
Pachapi sonqonsi kunununuchkan
chaynas mana wiksayuq machuypas katatan
kausay manaña tukuy rumi qina kaptin.
Usiapas chayna kaspas llaqtakunata waqtapayan
paratapas mana yajuyuqta saqespa
uywakunapas chakrakunapas wañuchkan
sachakunapas qerispa urpi qinas
rapinkunata rapapaspa
pampaman
chakraman wichin
chay chakrakunas manaña waytarinqachu
kikin runa allpapi llinkupi
kikimpa kausaynin wañuynin ñaupamanta ruaspa
wañuchkaq parapa weqenta mana sayanchitinqa.

*Tormenta

2

Pachapis runakuna ñakarin
yawarchasqa makimpiñataqsi
mana reqsipa apu qespirimun
wawa kayninñataqsi ñankunapi puriykachan
partin tantata maskaspa,
chaynas wamanikuna
orqupi machu condurkuna kaspa
pachatapas,
     sachakunatapas,
rumikunatas tusuchichkanku
mayu ukumanta qespirimuq qapariywan.
Runakunas urpikunawan
qatun pachapi tukuy kaqwansi
llakikunatas takiachin,
qanay pachas kuyutiaspa
uyanta kausay sachaspa colorninwan pintapakuspa
para qina
wamanpa ñawinman
rauraq rumita wichichimuptin
qanan pachapi kutirispas
lluptin.

3

Allpas manañas mosoqñachu
chaynas manaña ñoqanchikpachu
pillpintukunapa waqasqan pukiupis
urpikuna llakinta saqechkan.
Wauqey uyariy
        manañas waqay punchauñachu
machu taintanchikunapa rimariyninta uyariy
orqumanpa kikin sonqumantas qaparimuchkanku
amaña anchata waqaychu
sonqonsi nanan
ritipi qapariq cundurpa qinas
sonqoy nanan
maynas pampa kuyaq turu
wañuyta munan chay pampan saqenantaqa
chaynas sonqoy nanan
qam qinas pachapa apun
yarqaymanta, yakumanta wañuq wikuñapa
qaqte yawarnin manaña upiay munaq.
Wauqey uyariy
        manañas waqay punchauñachu
allpan ñoqanchikpa uqtawan kanqa
paranchiksi qamuchkanña,
chaynas llakinchikpas qamuchkan
qori kausay challwata apamuspa
machu taytanchikuna
qaway pachapi uqtawan tusunampaq.

5

Llaqtaykita kutirimusi manañas
kanmanchu paya sara
parawan pukllaspas tukuchkaq punchaywan asiyman
condurpa ripusqanta qawaspa
llakinkaq apu kasqaykimantas
kokapi llakikita upallachinki
qanaq pachapa uyampi urpikuna ruasqaykimanta.
Noqapa kasqanta manaña maskaymanñachu
chaynas mamaipa millqaynimpi tiyayta atiniñachu
llapa sonqukunapi tutuyaq chayamuyninta suyaspa
llaquiq apu kasqaykimantas
rapraykita rapapachinki mayupi
puyukunapi llakita cheqerichiptiki
wawa kasqayta maskani
kikin mana tukuq miski yakuykipi
imainam sachapa urpipa ukumanta illarirqani.

PORFIRIO MENESES LAZON
(Huanta, Ayacucho, 1915)

Porfirio Meneses Lazón is a writer and professor at the Universidad Federico Villarreal in Lima. He received two awards for his works in Spanish—the Juegos Florales de San Marcos Prize (1947) and the Premio Nacional de Fomento a la Cultura Ricardo Palma (1965). His poems in Quechua have been published in the anthology *Homenaje al Sesquicentenario de las Batallas de Junín y Ayacucho. Antología de la literatura quechua* (Lima: Editorial Nueva Educación, 1974), and in his collection *Suyaypa llaqtan/País de la esperanza* (Lima: Mosca Azul Editores, 1988), which is a compilation of his poetry in Quechua and Spanish translation. His poetry has also appeared in the literary journal *Runa* (Journal of the Instituto Nacional de Cultura, No. 1, Lima, 1977).

¿QUIEN?

¿Quién ronda, felino,
mi humilde chozuela
de miseria y espinos?

¿Quién da a la noche
mirar de serpiente?

¿Quién hace del silencio
letal cuchillo escondido?

¡Aunque no lo quiera,
aquí,
pozo de soledad y olvido,
sólo un atado de penas guardo!

WHO?

Who prowls like a cat
around my humble hut
of thorns and poverty?

Who gives the night
a serpent's gaze?

Who makes a lethal hidden knife
from silence?

No matter what,
here,
pit of solitude and oblivion,
A bundle of grief is all I hold!

VETE YA, SEÑOR

En nombre de la piedra
te hablo, señor.
Aquí muere tu soberbia.

La luna es nuestra, y su luz
es más hermosa
sobre nuestros sueños.

La nube es nuestra,
nos enjuga las sienes
en la brega de los días.

Y el sol, el sol
—mariposa de tiempo y oro—
descubre el alma de las cosas
y nos siembra
de flechas y rumbos
el corazón.

Nuestra es la tierra.
Vete ya, señor.

GET OUT, SEÑOR

In the name of the stone
I'm speaking to you, Señor.
Here's where your arrogance ends.

The moon is ours and her light
is more beautiful
above our dreams.

The clouds are ours
rinsing our brows
in the daily struggle.

Ah sun, the sun
—butterfly of time and gold—
uncovers the soul of things
sowing our hearts
with arrows
and paths.

The land is ours.
Get out, Señor!

PREGONERO AGRESTE

Canta el gallo aldeano
y es áureo pendón que flamea
el día en su pico.

Anuncia, severo,
la buena y mala valija del tiempo
viajero.

En la obsidiana de sus ojos,
fiero gusano de su cuello,
se eriza la vida.

Que existimos
un día más,
nos dice su canto.

RUSTIC CRIER

The village cock crows
and the day is unfurled,
a golden banner in his beak.

Starkly proclaiming
the traveling time
of a good or bad
bundle of news.

Life bristles
in obsidian eyes
and his neck is a golden worm.

His song rings out.
We exist
one more day.

SANDALIA DE INDIAS

Entonces, sandalia.
Entonces, abarca trizadora de distancias.
Entonces, y siempre, flor:
los caminos acogen tu huella
de lumbre y simiente.

Un afán se hace verbo
en cada paso, el tiempo
viene a ti como blanda ola
y es música
de corazón empecinado, de reloj,
de viento,
y a veces y siempre,
de angustia.

Otros cielos, niebla y aire,
besaron tus cordeles,
ojota maravillosa;
tú le das alada sombra
al río inerte del camino,
y hay en cada montaña
¡un pedestal para tu empeño!

INDIAN WOMAN'S SANDAL

So, sandal,
So, mower of distance,
So, and always, flower,
roads hold your footstep
of light and seed.

Toil becomes word
at each step, time
fits you like a gentle wave
and is music
of the stubborn heart,
of the clock, the wind
and sometimes and always,
anguish.

Other skies, mist and air
kissed your straps,
wonderful rough sandal;
you spread winged shade
across the still river of road
and on each mountain
there's a step for your thrust!

¿PIM CHAY?*

¿Pim chay . . . ?
¿Ima usqutaq muyupayamun
kay wakcha,
kichkasapa chukllallayta?

¿Pim tutayaqman
maqta urupa ñawinta
churamun?

¿Pitaq chay,
muyuriyniypi
chun niqmanta
samka tumi r999ruraruq kachkan?

¡Mana munastinpas,
kaypi,
sapan kaypa, qunqaypa
quchanpi,
llaki qipillatam uywani!

*¿Quién?

RIPUYÑA, TAYTA*

Rumi rantinpim rimayki, tayta.
Kaypim puchukan
apukachasqayki.

Ñuqaykupam killa, kanchayninmi
aswanta sumaqyakun
musquyniyku pitusqampi.

Puyupas ñuqaykupam;
humpiykutam pichawanku
sapa punchaw atipaykuypi.

Intipas, intipas,
—wiña wiñaypaq kawsaq
quri pillpintu—,
llapa imap ukunta rikurichin
hinaspan
may rinaykuta, wachikumata
sunquykupi muyawanku.

Kikiykupam allpa.
Ripuyña, tayta.

*Vete ya señor

QAPARIKU*

Tupsampi,
quri latapata hina
achikyayta rapapachistin,
chusu llaqtapi utululla
takikun.

Manchaypaq willarikun
imapas allin mana allin
unarayaypa
wallqarikamusqanta.

Sinchi qispi ñawinkunapi,
piñarikuq askankuy
kunkampi,
chutarikun kawsay.

Huk punchawraq
kawsakusqanchiktam niwanchik
takimpi.

*Pregonero agreste

PAQU KITIKUNAPA USUTAN*

Hinaptinchu, siquylla;
hinaptinchu, karu watiqaykuna ñutuchiq.
Hinaptinchu ñawpaqpas, wiñaypas, tika:
ñankunaman añachikunku
kanchaq, muyaq yupiykiwan.

Huk chamaymi sinchi runayan
sapa yupipi, kawsay mitañataq,
unarayay,
hamusunki
quchap qatanpi yakup qaspakuynin hina;
chaymanta,
ima churasqaykipas takim,
wañupakuq sunqupa takiynin,
inti watanapa, wayrapawan takin;
wakin mitakunapa, wiñaypa,
putisqa takin.

Huk rikchaq hanaq pachakunam,
puyu wayrakuna,
watuykita mucharqanku llipipiq usutallay;
qanmi raprayuq llantuta qunki
qasi chutarayaq mayu hina
ñanman;
chaymi sapa urqupas, hirkapas,
atipakuyniykipaq usnu churakun.

*Sandalia de indias

BIBLIOGRAPHY

Aguirre García, Dida. *Arcilla*. Lima: Lluvia Editores, 1989.

Flores Palomino, Lily. *Waqalliq-takin/Tañido de campanas*. Lima: CONCYTEC, 1989.

―――. *Phawaq titi*. Lima: Editorial Perú, 1985.

―――. *Troj de poemas quechua castellano*. Lima: César Lanegra, 1971.

Hurtado de Mendoza, William. *Pacha Yachachiq*. Lima: Universidad Agraria La Molina, 1992.

―――. *Poesía quechua*. Lima: Lluvia Editores, 1990.

―――. *Yachanaykipaq taki/Canción para que aprendas*, Lima: Perugraph Editores, 1997.

―――. *Yanapaq jailli*. Lima: Ediciones Martínez, 1971.

Meneses Lazón, Porfirio. *Suyaypa llaqtan/País de la esperanza*. Lima: Mozca Azul Editores, 1998.

Ninamango Mallqui, Eduardo. *Pukutay*. Lima: Tarea, 1982.

BIOGRAPHICAL INFORMATION

Julio Noriega Bernuy (Editor)
is the editor of the comprehensive anthology *Poesía quechua escrita en el Perú* (Lima: Centro de Estudios y Publicaciones, 1993), which features selections in Spanish and Quechua; and *Buscando una tradición poética quechua en el Perú* (Miami: University of Miami/North-South Center Press, 1995), which was awarded the Letras de Oro Literary Prize in 1995. He is Assistant Professor of Spanish American literature at the University of Notre Dame.

Maureen Ahern (Translator)
is a graduate of the National University of San Marcos, in Lima. She co-edited *Haravec*, a bilingual journal published in Peru in the 1960s, which included trilingual selections of Quechua poetry. Her translations of work by Antonio Cisneros and other contemporary Peruvian poets have been widely anthologized in the United States and England. She is a Professor of colonial and contemporary Andean and Mexican literatures at The Ohio State University in Columbus.

Daniel Shapiro (General Series Editor)
is Director of Literature and Managing Editor of *Review: Latin American Literature and Arts* at the Americas Society in New York. He is the author of an unpublished manuscript, "The Red Handkerchief and Other Poems," and is presently translating *Cipango*, by Chilean poet Tomás Harris. A selection of these translations appeared as the cover feature of the September/October 1997 issue of *The American Poetry Review*.